NICKELODEON

降去神通
AVATAR
THE LEGEND OF AANG

# THE ULTIMATE
# POCKET
# GUIDE

Based on the TV series *Nickelodeon Avatar: The Legend of Aang*™
as seen on Nickelodeon

First published in Great Britain in 2008 by Simon & Schuster UK Ltd
Africa House, 64–78 Kingsway, London WC2B 6AH
A CBS Company

Originally published in the USA in 2007 by Simon Spotlight,
an imprint of Simon & Schuster Children's Division, New York

A CIP catalogue record for this book is available from the British Library

ISBN-13: 978-1-84738-121-7

Printed in China

10 9 8 7 6 5 4 3 2 1

Visit our websites: www.simonsays.co.uk
www.nick.co.uk

Additional illustrations by Patrick Spaziante and Shane L. Johnson

# THE ULTIMATE POCKET GUIDE

by Tom Mason and Dan Danko

Simon and Schuster/Nickelodeon

# NATION: **The Air Nomads**

*LOCATION:* The Air Nomads lived in four temples, all of which are at high altitudes. You can only reach them by flying. There are temples located at each compass point— north, south, east, and west.

*HISTORY:* The Air Nomads were considered the most mysterious of all the benders because they were wiped out one hundred years ago by the Fire Nation, therefore not much is known about their culture. Fire Lord Sozin started the war when Avatar Roku died, and he wanted to stop the new Avatar from being born.

# The Monks

The Air Nomads were led by an order of monks. They preferred to use their powers strictly for defensive purposes. The monks, especially Monk Gyatso, were responsible for training the new Avatar.

Despite their strict morals, Air Nomads still knew how to have fun. Two of their favorite pastimes were sky bison polo and airball.

*SKY BISON POLO:* Sky bison polo was played in the air. Airbenders rode upon their flying bison and tried to force a ball into an opponent's goal. Championship matches were held at the Northern Air Temple.

*AIRBALL:* This was a traditional Air Nomad game that relied on an Airbender's speed, balance, and accuracy. It was an extremely fast-paced game where players on two teams used Airbending to pass the ball from one player to another. The goal was to get the ball through the wooden ring on an opponent's side.

**DID YOU KNOW?** MANY OF THE MONKS WERE EXCELLENT BAKERS!

NAME: **Aang**

AGE: 112 YEARS OLD

NATION: AIR NOMADS

UNFORGETTABLE TRAIT: AANG IS THE AVATAR. HE CAN AIRBEND, WATERBEND, EARTHBEND, AND FIREBEND.

**A**ang is the 112-year-old boy that the current incarnation of the Avatar Spirit was born into.

He spent the last one hundred years trapped in an iceberg at the South Pole. He was set free by Katara and her brother, Sokka, who were also the first people to tell him about the one-hundred-year-old war between the Fire Nation and the other three nations.

**DID YOU KNOW?** THE ARROW DESIGN ON AANG'S HEAD IS A TATTOO! ALL AIRBENDERS GET TATTOOED WHEN THEY MASTER AIRBENDING.

**SECRET FACT:** AANG WASN'T SUPPOSED TO BE TOLD THAT HE WAS THE AVATAR UNTIL THE AGE OF SIXTEEN, BUT WHEN THE MONKS SENSED THE THREAT TO THE BALANCE OF THE NATIONS, THEY MADE AN EXCEPTION.

**CHECK IT OUT:** AANG'S WOODEN STAFF IS AN OLD AND PRECIOUS GIFT FROM THE MONKS. HE SOMETIMES USES IT AS A GLIDER.

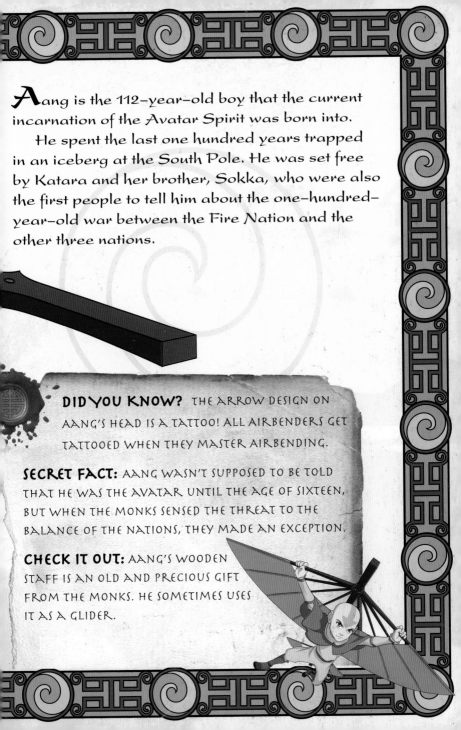

# NAME: **Appa**

**NATION:** AIR NOMADS

**UNFORGETTABLE TRAIT:**
APPA'S ALSO AN AIRBENDER.

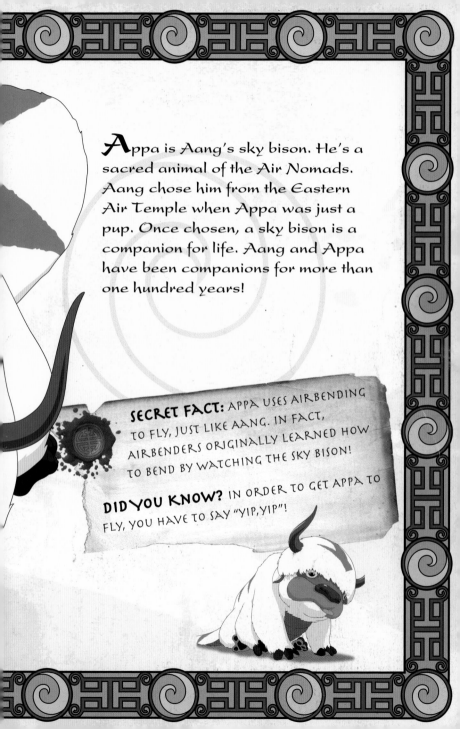

Appa is Aang's sky bison. He's a sacred animal of the Air Nomads. Aang chose him from the Eastern Air Temple when Appa was just a pup. Once chosen, a sky bison is a companion for life. Aang and Appa have been companions for more than one hundred years!

**SECRET FACT:** APPA USES AIRBENDING TO FLY, JUST LIKE AANG. IN FACT, AIRBENDERS ORIGINALLY LEARNED HOW TO BEND BY WATCHING THE SKY BISON!

**DID YOU KNOW?** IN ORDER TO GET APPA TO FLY, YOU HAVE TO SAY "YIP, YIP"!

NAME: **Monk Gyatso**

**NATION:** AIR NOMADS

**UNFORGETTABLE TRAIT:**
MONK GYATSO TRAINED
AANG IN AIRBENDING.

**A** powerful Airbender,
Monk Gyatso lived at
the Southern Air Temple
and taught Airbending.
He believed in keeping
the world in peace and
harmony, and used
Airbending only for
defensive purposes. He
was probably the greatest
Airbender in the world. Monk Gyatso revealed to
Aang that he was the Avatar when he was twelve
years old.

**DID YOU KNOW?** MONK GYATSO WAS AN
EXCELLENT BAKER WHO MADE DELICIOUS FRUIT PIES!

**SECRET FACT:** MONK GYATSO TAUGHT AANG HOW TO
PLAY A GAME CALLED *PAI SHO*, AND THEY USED TO PLAY
WHENEVER THEY TOOK A BREAK FROM TRAINING. MONK
GYATSO ALSO LIKES TO CHEAT!

NAME: **Momo**

**NATION:** AIR NOMADS

**UNFORGETTABLE TRAIT:** MOMO CAN'T SPEAK, BUT HE CAN AND WILL EAT EVERYTHING IN SIGHT.

**M**omo is a winged lemur that Aang found at the Jongmu Air Temple when he went there to look for Monk Gyatso.

A winged lemur is a traditional Airbender pet.

Momo has incredible senses of hearing and smell. He can alert the gang to danger from miles away, a skill that definitely comes in handy!

**DID YOU KNOW?** MOMO'S FAVORITE HOBBY IS EATING. AND HE LOVES TO EAT ANYTHING THAT SOKKA EATS!

**SECRET FACT:** "MOMO" MEANS "PEACH" IN JAPANESE.

# THE AVATAR STATE

**T**he Avatar State is triggered whenever Aang is in an extreme physical or emotional state. Unfortunately Aang can't control himself while he's in it—not yet anyway.

When he's entering the Avatar State, his eyes turn white-hot and his tattoos pulse and glow.

All the Avatars share one spirit, so the ones who came before Aang help him, usually by adding strength and power to his bending skills.

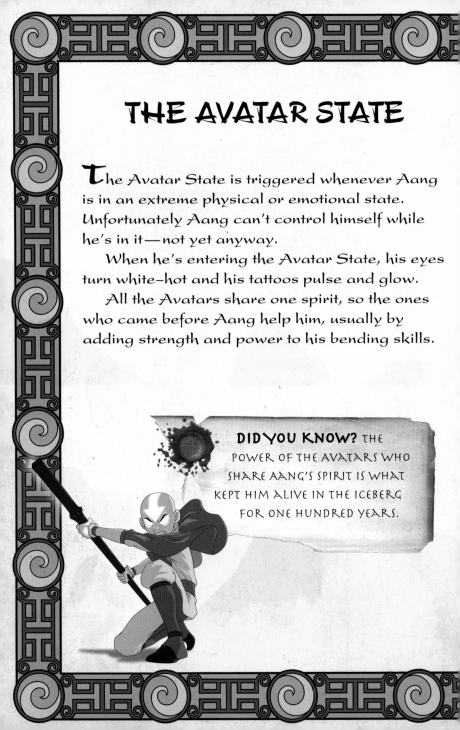

**DID YOU KNOW?** THE POWER OF THE AVATARS WHO SHARE AANG'S SPIRIT IS WHAT KEPT HIM ALIVE IN THE ICEBERG FOR ONE HUNDRED YEARS.

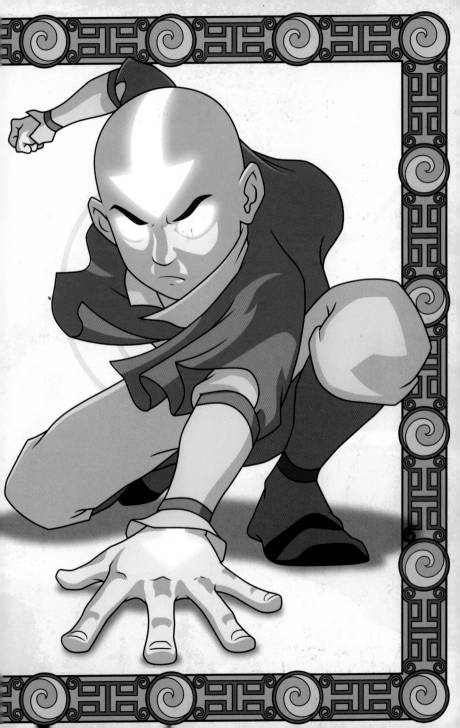

# THE SPIRIT WORLD

The Spirit World exists alongside the everyday physical world, but very few people have the ability to see it. Spirit creatures live in the Spirit World and act as guardians of the rivers, forests, and mountains.

As the Avatar, Aang can enter the Spirit World, but no one in the physical world can see or hear the spirit version of himself when he's there.

There is one major danger: If his physical body is moved while his spirit is in the Spirit World, his spirit might not find its way back to his physical body! That's already happened to Aang a few times; mainly it's been Prince Zuko's fault.

## DID YOU KNOW?
BENDING DOESN'T WORK IN THE SPIRIT WORLD!

# NATION: The Water Tribes

**LOCATION:** There are two Water Tribes. The Southern Water Tribe lives at the South Pole while the Northern Water Tribe lives at the North Pole.

**HISTORY:** The Northern and Southern Water Tribes used to be united as one tribe. But the group split into two following their inability to agree on certain social and cultural practices, and a group of Waterbenders journeyed to the South Pole to start a new life.

# Southern Water Tribe

At first they lived much like the Northern Tribe; with walled cities made of ice and a modern civilization. But when the Fire Nation war broke out, the men of the Southern Water Tribe went to fight, and much of the Southern Water Tribe was destroyed.

# Northern Water Tribe

The city of the Northern Water Tribe remained intact, and is ruled by Chief Arnook. He has a rule about not teaching women to Waterbend—but Katara was the first woman to make him break that rule by showing Master Pakku, the Waterbending master, that she was skilled enough to fight.

**DID YOU KNOW?** WATER TRIBE KIDS LOVE PENGUIN SLEDDING, WHICH IS RIDING THE BACK OF A PENGUIN DOWN AN ICY HILL!

# NAME: **Katara**

**AGE:** 14 YEARS OLD

**NATION:**
SOUTHERN
WATER
TRIBE

**UNFORGETTABLE TRAIT:** KATARA IS A SKILLED WATERBENDER, THE ONLY WATERBENDER IN THE SOUTHERN WATER TRIBE.

Katara practices Waterbending every day and is very disciplined. Katara's mother was a healer and herbalist. Katara has inherited some of her mother's abilities. When the gang went to the North Pole, Yagoda—a healing master—taught Katara how to heal by using Waterbending.

Katara and Sokka's mother died when they were young. Their father, Hakoda, left the South Pole with the other men of the tribe to fight the Fire Nation.

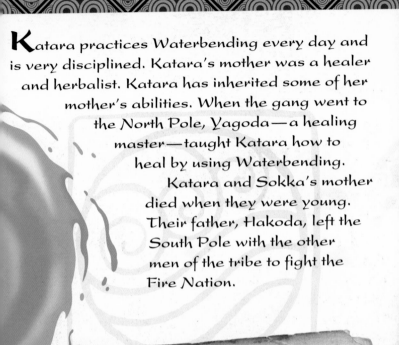

**DID YOU KNOW?** KATARA ALWAYS WEARS THE NECKLACE THAT HER MOTHER GAVE HER AROUND HER NECK.

**CHECK IT OUT:** KATARA'S NECKLACE WAS ACTUALLY A BETROTHAL NECKLACE THAT MASTER PAKKU MADE FOR KATARA'S GRANDMOTHER!

# NAME: **Sokka**

**AGE:** 15 YEARS OLD

**NATION:**
SOUTHERN
WATER TRIBE

**UNFORGETTABLE TRAIT:**
SOKKA IS A GREAT
WARRIOR, AND HE'S
ALMOST ALWAYS THE
MAN WITH THE PLAN.

Sokka's most prized possession is his boomerang, a traditional Water Tribe weapon that was given to him by his father.

Unlike his younger sister, Sokka doesn't have any bending abilities. Sokka can sometimes act like a real goofball, but he really cares about his family and friends, and would do anything to protect them. He's also quite the ladies' man.

**DID YOU KNOW?** SOKKA'S ACTUALLY HAPPY HE DOESN'T HAVE A BENDING SKILL. HE'D RATHER DEFEAT THE FIRE NATION WITH HIS BARE BRAWN AND WARRIOR TACTICS.

**CHECK IT OUT:** WHEN THE GANG WAS ATTACKED BY CANYON CRAWLERS IN THE GREAT DIVIDE, SOKKA KNOCKED ONE OF THE CREATURES WITH HIS BOOMERANG TO DRAW THE CREATURES' ATTENTION TOWARD HIMSELF AND AWAY FROM THE INJURED GUIDE.

# NATION: The Fire Nation

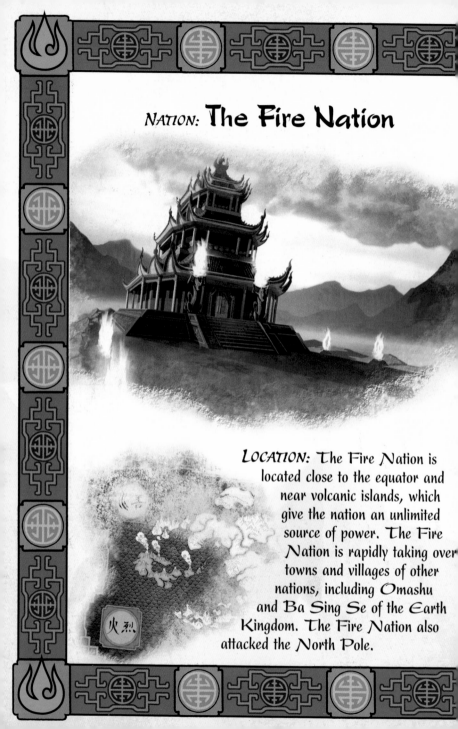

**LOCATION:** The Fire Nation is located close to the equator and near volcanic islands, which give the nation an unlimited source of power. The Fire Nation is rapidly taking over towns and villages of other nations, including Omashu and Ba Sing Se of the Earth Kingdom. The Fire Nation also attacked the North Pole.

**HISTORY:** The Fire Nation used to live in peace with the other nations until Fire Lord Sozin came to rule. Since then, the leaders of the Fire Nation have been driven by a single goal: to destroy the other three nations and conquer the world.

**DID YOU KNOW?** A SOLAR ECLIPSE TEMPORARILY TAKES AWAY A FIREBENDER'S POWER BECAUSE THE SUN IS HIDDEN BEHIND THE MOON. FIREBENDERS CAN'T BEND WITHOUT THE HEAT AND ENERGY FROM THE SUN.

NAMES: **Fire Lord Sozin**
and his grandson **Ozai**

**NATION:** FIRE NATION

**UNFORGETTABLE TRAITS:** THIS GRANDFATHER-AND-GRANDSON TEAM IS A PAIR OF RUTHLESS TYRANTS.

**F**ire Lord Sozin had been secretly plotting the war while Avatar Roku, the Avatar before Aang, was still alive. The Avatar's reincarnation follows a cycle—Water, Earth, Fire, Air—so the next Avatar was bound to come from the Air Nomads. Once Avatar Roku died, Sozin attacked the Air Nomads to try to keep the Avatar from reincarnating.

Sozin wanted to create a world where Fire existed as the dominant element, and no nation could challenge his rule. He used the heat from a passing comet to attack all four nations at once. The comet is now called Sozin's Comet and returns every one hundred years.

**DID YOU KNOW?** SOZIN'S COMET IS COMING BACK AT THE END OF THE SUMMER, AND OZAI PLANS TO USE ITS STRENGTH TO WIN THE WAR ONCE AND FOR ALL.

**O**zai is the current Fire Lord and the grandson of Fire Lord Sozin. He is carrying on the war his grandfather started. He's very dangerous, and he'll stop at nothing in his quest for world domination—just like his grandfather.

**DID YOU KNOW?** DESPITE THE FACT THAT OZAI WAS YOUNGER THAN HIS BROTHER, IROH, HE MANAGED TO USURP THE POSITION OF FIRE LORD FROM HIS OLDER BROTHER.

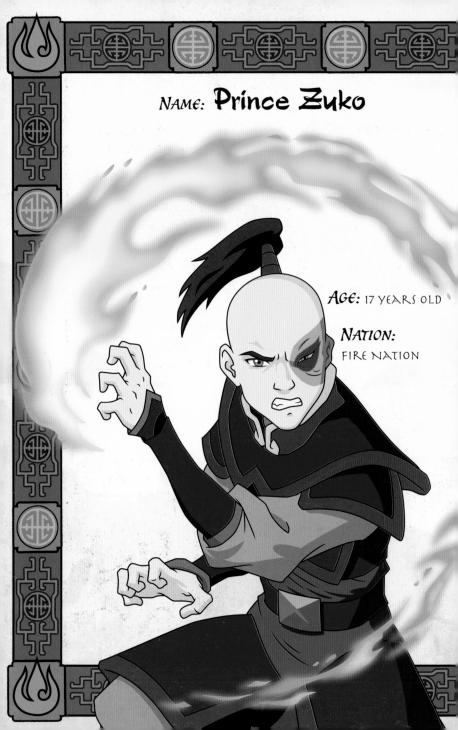

NAME: **Prince Zuko**

AGE: 17 YEARS OLD

NATION:
FIRE NATION

**UNFORGETTABLE TRAIT:** ZUKO HAS A SCAR ON HIS FACE FROM A BURN THAT WAS GIVEN TO HIM BY HIS FATHER AS A RESULT OF A FIGHT.

**P**rince Zuko is the eldest son of Fire Lord Ozai. Zuko had publicly disagreed with his father about his plan for global conquest, so his father challenged him to an *Agni Kai*, a traditional Firebender duel. He was badly scarred and exiled from his home.

In order to return to the Fire Nation and reclaim his birthright, Zuko must bring the Avatar to his father to prove his honor.

**DID YOU KNOW?** PRINCE ZUKO ONCE DISGUISED HIMSELF AS THE BLUE SPIRIT TO RESCUE AANG FROM ADMIRAL ZHAO'S FORTRESS. BUT HE ONLY FREED AANG SO THAT HE COULD HAVE THE AVATAR TO HIMSELF AND REGAIN HIS HONOR.

NAME: **Princess Azula**

**AGE:** 14 YEARS OLD

**NATION:** FIRE NATION

**UNFORGETTABLE TRAIT:** PRINCESS AZULA IS THREE YEARS YOUNGER THAN HER BROTHER, ZUKO, BUT A FAR MORE ADVANCED FIREBENDER. HER CLAIM TO FAME IS FIREBENDING LIGHTNING.

$S$purred by her older brother's failure to capture the Avatar, she decided to do it herself, not only to prove how capable she is, but how much of a failure her brother is as well. And while she was at it, she also tried to invade the walled city of Ba Sing Se, capital of the Earth Kingdom, a task that her Uncle Iroh failed to do years ago.

According to Zuko, Azula is full of lies and deceit.

Azula has two girlfriends she's enlisted for help: Ty Lee and Mai. Ty Lee is a performer in a small circus. Mai's father was appointed governor of Omashu by Fire Lord Ozai. All three girls attended the Royal Fire Academy for Girls.

**DID YOU KNOW?** AZULA TEASES ZUKO BY CALLING HIM "ZU-ZU."

**CHECK IT OUT:** THE MOST DANGEROUS FIREBENDING FLAME IS LIGHTNING. THE PUREST FORM OF FIREBENDING, IT IS WITHOUT ANGER OR EMOTIONS. SOMETIMES IT IS REFERRED TO AS "COLD-BLOODED FIRE" BECAUSE IT IS SO FIERCE THAT TO CREATE IT, THE FIREBENDER MUST BE COMPLETELY CALM AND COLD-HEARTED TOWARD HIS OR HER

**NAME: Iroh**

**NATION:** FIRE NATION

**UNFORGETTABLE TRAIT:** IROH HAS A GREAT SENSE OF HUMOR, AND CARES VERY MUCH ABOUT HIS NEPHEW, PRINCE ZUKO. IROH IS ALSO AN AVID TEA LOVER.

Iroh was the firstborn son of Azulon, son of Sozin, which makes Ozai his younger brother. He is a former general and war hero of the Fire Nation. Not a fan of her Uncle Iroh, Princess Azula often underestimates the powerful Firebending skills he still retains.

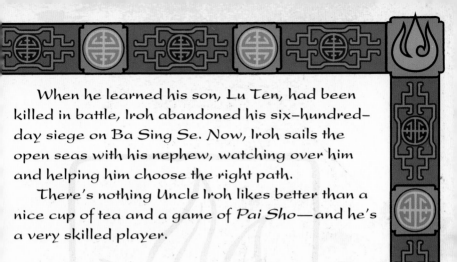

When he learned his son, Lu Ten, had been killed in battle, Iroh abandoned his six-hundred-day siege on Ba Sing Se. Now, Iroh sails the open seas with his nephew, watching over him and helping him choose the right path.

There's nothing Uncle Iroh likes better than a nice cup of tea and a game of *Pai Sho*—and he's a very skilled player.

**PAI SHO:** *PAI SHO* IS AN ANCIENT TILE GAME THAT'S PLAYED IN ALL FOUR NATIONS. CERTAIN *PAI SHO* PLAYERS ARE MEMBERS OF A SPECIAL ORDER CALLED THE WHITE LOTUS—A SECRET ORGANIZATION OF MEMBERS FROM ALL FOUR NATIONS.

**DID YOU KNOW?** IROH IS ALSO KNOWN AS "THE DRAGON OF THE WEST" BECAUSE HE CAN FIREBEND WITH HIS MOUTH.

## NAME: **Avatar Roku**

**NATION:** FIRE NATION

**UNFORGETTABLE TRAIT:**
ROKU WAS THE AVATAR
WHO CAME BEFORE
AANG; HE WAS
THE ONLY ONE TO
STAND UP TO FIRE
LORD SOZIN.

**A**vatar Roku
was first and
foremost a
Firebender.
When he was
alive, he kept
the four nations
living in peace and
harmony.

Roku's home was the Fire Temple, which
he built on an active volcanic island named

Crescent Island. It's deep
in Fire Nation territory and
guarded by Fire Sages. The
Fire Sages used to be loyal
to the Avatar, but now they
are loyal to Ozai.

Crescent Island is where Aang met and spoke to Avatar Roku's spirit for the first time.

**CHECK IT OUT:** ROKU'S DRAGON IS A POWERFUL ANIMAL SPIRIT THAT HE USES TO SEND VISIONS TO AANG.

# Colonel Mongke and the Rough Rhinos

An elite group of Fire Nation Cavalry, the Rough Rhinos specialize in raiding the Earth Kingdom. Their leader is Colonel Mongke. He's the only Firebender of the group.

Each member carries a very specialized weapon and they ride Komodo Rhinos.

When Iroh served in the Fire Nation Army, the Rough Rhinos used to work for him.

**DID YOU KNOW?** ACCORDING TO IROH, THE ROUGH RHINOS ARE ALSO A WELL-KNOWN SINGING GROUP.

# NAME: The Earth Kingdom

*LOCATION:* A huge land mass in the eastern hemisphere.

*HISTORY:* The Earth Kingdom is the most powerful nation, with the exception of the Fire Nation. The Earth King lives in the walled city of Ba Sing Se, which means "the Great Impenetrable City." However, up until recently, the Earth Kingdom was actually ruled by the evil Long Feng and his spies, the Dai Li. They were the king's royal enforcers. The king didn't even know about the war until the gang finally convinced him it had been going on for a century!

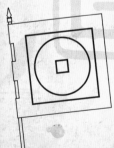

*OMASHU:* King Bumi rules the second largest city in the Earth Kingdom. The only way to get there is by walking a long, narrow path over a dangerous chasm. Or you could fly. When the Fire Nation conquered Omashu, Princess Azula changed its name to New Ozai.

**BA SING SE:** This is the capital city of the Earth Kingdom and home of the ruler, the Earth King. The city has been under attack from the Fire Nation many times during the war. Its many walls have protected it so far.

**KYOSHI ISLAND:** Located in the South Sea, Kyoshi Island is part of the Earth Kingdom and is named for the Avatar who was born there four hundred years ago. Avatar Kyoshi created Kyoshi Island to protect it from an evil Earth king. Each village has a leader and a band of female Kyoshi warriors. None of them are Earthbenders, but they're still excellent fighters!

**SANDBENDERS:** Sandbenders are Earthbending nomads who live in the desert of the Earth Kingdom and know how to bend sand.

**DID YOU KNOW?** A FAVORITE METHOD OF TRANSPORTATION IN THE EARTH KINGDOM IS THE OSTRICH HORSE.

**CHECK IT OUT:** SANDBENDERS SAIL THE DESERT IN SANDSAILERS.

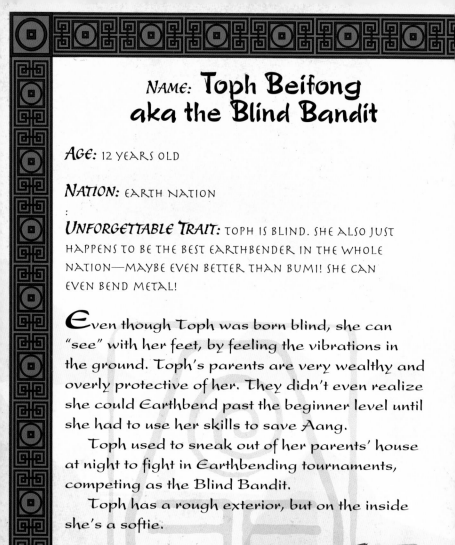

# NAME: Toph Beifong
# aka the Blind Bandit

**AGE:** 12 YEARS OLD

**NATION:** EARTH NATION

**UNFORGETTABLE TRAIT:** TOPH IS BLIND. SHE ALSO JUST HAPPENS TO BE THE BEST EARTHBENDER IN THE WHOLE NATION—MAYBE EVEN BETTER THAN BUMI! SHE CAN EVEN BEND METAL!

Even though Toph was born blind, she can "see" with her feet, by feeling the vibrations in the ground. Toph's parents are very wealthy and overly protective of her. They didn't even realize she could Earthbend past the beginner level until she had to use her skills to save Aang.

Toph used to sneak out of her parents' house at night to fight in Earthbending tournaments, competing as the Blind Bandit.

Toph has a rough exterior, but on the inside she's a softie.

**SECRET FACT:** TOPH HAS A BIG CRUSH ON SOKKA.

## NAME: **King Bumi**

### NATION: EARTH NATION

### UNFORGETTABLE TRAIT:
KING BUMI IS CRAZY! HE'S ALSO ONE HUNDRED AND TWELVE YEARS OLD, JUST LIKE AANG.

**A**ang and Bumi were friends when they were children, and now Bumi is the king of Omashu, which he recently surrendered to the Fire Nation. Although he doesn't look it at first, King Bumi is actually a really powerful Earthbender. He is also a trickster who loves messing with people and playing jokes on them.

**SECRET FACT:** FLOPSIE, KING BUMI'S PET, IS A GOAT GORILLA. HE SEEMS VICIOUS, BUT HE IS ACTUALLY QUITE LOVABLE AND DOCILE.

# Wan Shi Tong and his Legendary Library

The kids met Professor Zei on their vacation at the Oasis. He was searching for Wan Shi Tong's Library, which contains a vast collection of knowledge. He said the library was buried in the Si Wong Desert. The gang was searching for information on the Fire Nation, so they decided to go with him.

Wan Shi Tong is the Great Knowledge Spirit— "He Who Knows Ten Thousand Things." The Spirit takes the form of a giant owl! Inside the library, the kids found all sorts of information, including a calendar that could foretell when the next solar eclipse would be. This information is going to help them defeat the Fire Nation once and for all.

**CHECK IT OUT:** AANG DONATED A FIRE NATION WANTED POSTER OF HIMSELF TO THE LIBRARY'S COLLECTION.

# The Bending Arts

A bender's power comes from his or her internal life energy, or chi. Its limits are defined only by the skill, strength, and stamina of the bender.

*FIREBENDING:* Firebending is an aggressive and offensive fighting force, not a defensive one. A Firebender tries to overwhelm an opponent with a barrage of blows in a variety of moves.

**SECRET FACT:** A SHORT JAB CREATES A BURST OF FLAMES, WHILE A SPINNING KICK CREATES RINGS OF FIRE.

**FIREBENDER TO BEAT:** PRINCESS AZULA

*WATERBENDING:* Waterbenders use their chi to control water, like the way the moon controls the tides. By nature, Waterbending is a defensive art.

**SECRET FACT:** A WATERBENDER ALWAYS CARRIES A SKIN OF WATER WITH HIM OR HER, JUST IN CASE.

**WATERBENDER TO BEAT:** KATARA

*EARTHBENDING:* Earthbenders use the ground as a weapon against an opponent. An Earthbender can rupture the ground, manipulate the dirt, and levitate and hurl rocks.

**SECRET FACT:** THE HIGHEST LEVEL EARTHBENDERS CAN REDUCE SOLID ROCK TO QUICKSAND TO CAPTURE ENEMIES.

**EARTHBENDER TO BEAT:** TOPH

*AIRBENDING:* Airbending is also defensive, like Waterbending. An Airbender defends with blasts of wind, and then uses a variety of wind—based counterattacks to knock an opponent off his or her feet.

**SECRET FACT:** AIRBENDERS ARE FASTER AND MORE AGILE THAN ALL OTHER BENDERS.

**AIRBENDER TO BEAT:** AANG

# The Romance of Avatar

The world of Avatar is filled with secret romances and crushes, stolen glances, shy smiles, and an occasional kiss. Here's a handy way to keep track of who likes whom!

### Aang–Katara

Aang has had a crush on Katara since he first met her, but it's unclear if Katara feels the same way.

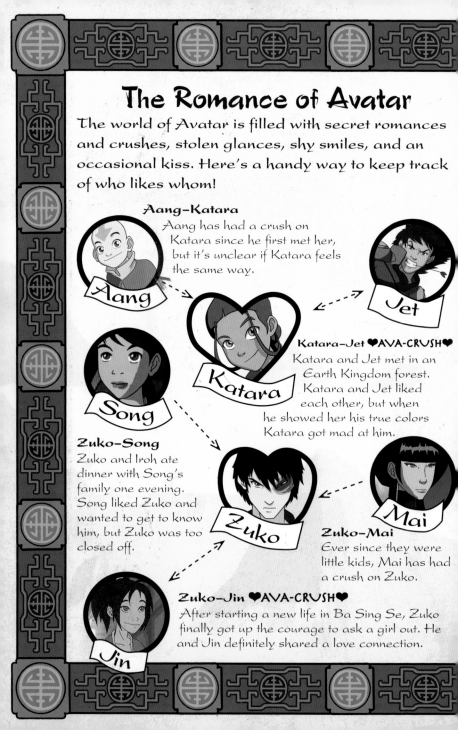

### Katara–Jet ♥AVA-CRUSH♥

Katara and Jet met in an Earth Kingdom forest. Katara and Jet liked each other, but when he showed her his true colors Katara got mad at him.

### Zuko–Song

Zuko and Iroh ate dinner with Song's family one evening. Song liked Zuko and wanted to get to know him, but Zuko was too closed off.

### Zuko–Mai

Ever since they were little kids, Mai has had a crush on Zuko.

### Zuko–Jin ♥AVA-CRUSH♥

After starting a new life in Ba Sing Se, Zuko finally got up the courage to ask a girl out. He and Jin definitely shared a love connection.

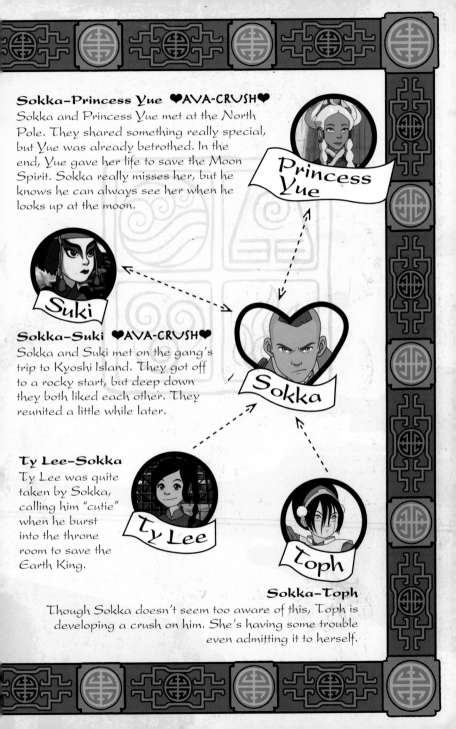

**Sokka–Princess Yue** ♥AVA-CRUSH♥
Sokka and Princess Yue met at the North Pole. They shared something really special, but Yue was already betrothed. In the end, Yue gave her life to save the Moon Spirit. Sokka really misses her, but he knows he can always see her when he looks up at the moon.

Princess Yue

Suki

**Sokka–Suki** ♥AVA-CRUSH♥
Sokka and Suki met on the gang's trip to Kyoshi Island. They got off to a rocky start, but deep down they both liked each other. They reunited a little while later.

Sokka

**Ty Lee–Sokka**
Ty Lee was quite taken by Sokka, calling him "cutie" when he burst into the throne room to save the Earth King.

Ty Lee

Toph

**Sokka–Toph**
Though Sokka doesn't seem too aware of this, Toph is developing a crush on him. She's having some trouble even admitting it to herself.

### THE AVATAR CHALLENGE
# Who Are You Most Like?

Are you more like Aang? Or Sokka? Or Katara?
Take the Avatar challenge and find out for
yourself.

## 1. IF YOU RUN OUT OF FOOD OR MONEY, WHAT'S THE FIRST THING YOU DO?

A. GO HUNTING
B. GET A JOB
C. COMPLAIN

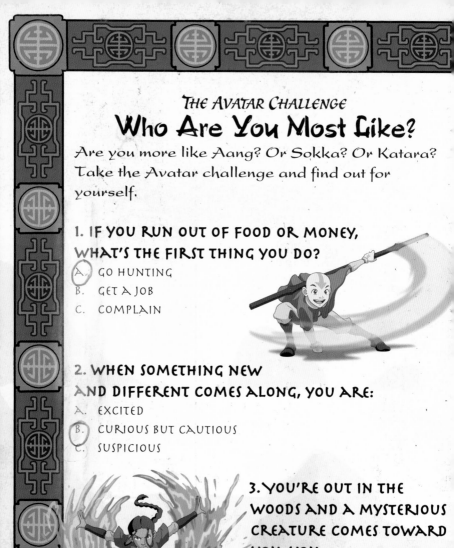

## 2. WHEN SOMETHING NEW AND DIFFERENT COMES ALONG, YOU ARE:

A. EXCITED
B. CURIOUS BUT CAUTIOUS
C. SUSPICIOUS

## 3. YOU'RE OUT IN THE WOODS AND A MYSTERIOUS CREATURE COMES TOWARD YOU. YOU:

A. WANT TO RIDE IT
B. COMMUNICATE WITH IT
C. PROTECT YOURSELF

## 4. WHEN A LARGE WALL

**BLOCKS YOUR ENTRANCE TO A CITY, YOU:**

A. JUMP OVER THE WALL
B. KNOCK ON THE DOOR AND WAIT FOR AN ANSWER
C. WANT TO GO HOME

**5. THE ENEMY IS GOING TO ATTACK THE VILLAGE OF A FRIEND. WHAT WOULD YOU DO?**

A. RUSH OUT TO FIGHT THEM
B. MAKE PREPARATIONS FOR A LONG FIGHT
C. COME UP WITH A BATTLE STRATEGY

**6. IF A BULLY WAS BOTHERING YOU, YOU WOULD:**

A. TURN HIS POWER AGAINST HIM
B. FIND OUT WHAT WAS REALLY BOTHERING HIM
C. STAND YOUR GROUND AND STAND UP FOR YOURSELF

**7. IF YOU COULD BE AN ANIMAL, YOU WOULD WANT TO BE:**

A. A BIRD
B. A FISH
C. "WHO WANTS TO BE AN ANIMAL?"

# 8. IF SOMEONE ASKS IF YOU'RE THE AVATAR, YOU:

A. SAY YES RIGHT AWAY
B. TRY TO FIGURE OUT WHY THEY WANT TO KNOW
C. "WHY WOULD I WANT TO BE THE AVATAR?"

# 9. WHEN YOU'RE NOT TRAVELING, YOU LIKE TO:

A. MEDITATE
B. PRACTICE AND STUDY YOUR SKILLS
C. EAT

# 10. WHEN VISITING A NEW VILLAGE, YOU:

A. MAKE FRIENDS EASILY
B. TRY TO FIT IN
C. WEAR A DISGUISE

# 11. YOU'D LIKE TO SPEND MOST OF YOUR TIME:

A. IN THE AIR
B. IN THE WATER
C. ON THE GROUND

# 12. IF YOU COULD HAVE ONE WISH COME TRUE, WHAT WOULD IT BE?

A. FOR THE WORLD TO LIVE IN PEACE
B. TO BE ABLE TO SAVE EVERYONE IN NEED
C. TO HAVE A NEVER-ENDING SUPPLY OF FREE FOOD

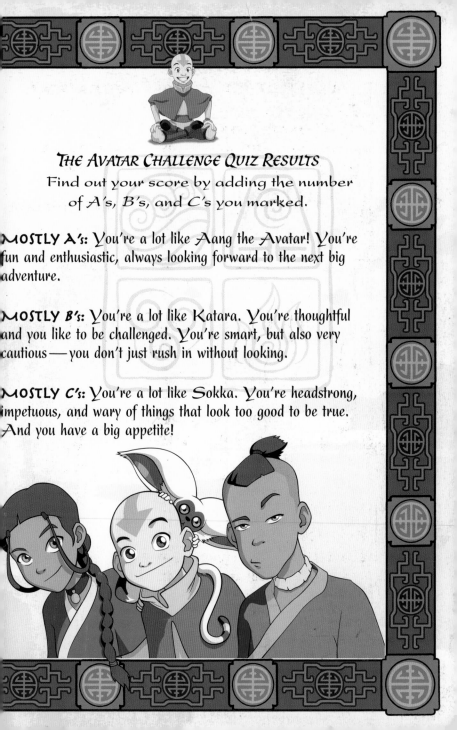

# THE AVATAR CHALLENGE QUIZ RESULTS

Find out your score by adding the number of A's, B's, and C's you marked.

**MOSTLY A's:** You're a lot like Aang the Avatar! You're fun and enthusiastic, always looking forward to the next big adventure.

**MOSTLY B's:** You're a lot like Katara. You're thoughtful and you like to be challenged. You're smart, but also very cautious—you don't just rush in without looking.

**MOSTLY C's:** You're a lot like Sokka. You're headstrong, impetuous, and wary of things that look too good to be true. And you have a big appetite!

# Who Said It?

**Aang**

**Uncle Iroh**

**Katara**

**Toph**

**Prince Zuko**

**Princess Azula**

**Sokka**

1. "I WANT MY HONOR, MY THRONE. I WANT MY FATHER NOT TO THINK I'M WORTHLESS!"

2. "YOU MEAN YOU HAVEN'T GUESSED? YOU DON'T SEE THE FAMILY RESEMBLANCE? HERE'S A HINT: 'I MUST FIND THE AVATAR TO RESTORE MY HONOR.' IT'S OKAY, YOU CAN LAUGH—IT'S FUNNY."

3. "THERE'S A RIGHT WAY TO DO THIS. PRACTICE, STUDY, DISCIPLINE."

4. "IF I HAD WEIRD POWERS, I'D KEEP MY 'WEIRDNESS' TO MYSELF."

5. "FOLLOW YOUR PASSION AND LIFE WILL REWARD YOU."

6. "IF YOU WANT TO BE A BENDER, YOU HAVE TO LET GO OF FEAR."

7. "YOU GUYS GET TO GO WHEREVER YOU WANT— NO ONE TELLING YOU WHAT TO DO. THAT'S THE LIFE. IT'S JUST NOT MY LIFE."

ANSWERS: 1. Prince Zuko / 2. Princess Azula / 3. Katara / 4. Sokka / 5. Uncle Iroh / 6. Aang / 7. Toph